Following Our Father
A Devotional for Dads

By Anthony Vandagriff

Foreword by Derrick Weeks

Table of Contents

A Path for Imperfect Dads 1
How to Use this Devotional 3
Our Father is Love 5
Our Father is Forgiving 9
Our Father is Gracious 13
Our Father is Faithful 17
Our Father is Just 21
Our Father is Creative 25
Our Father is a Provider 29
Our Father is a Teacher 33
Our Father is a Communicator 37
Our Father is Unchanging 41
Our Father is Proactive 45
Our Father is Everlasting 49
Our Father is Committed 53
Our Father is Honest 57
Our Father is a Servant 61
Our Father is an Example 65
Our Father is a Comforter 69
Our Father is Selfless 73
Our Father is Principled 77
Our Father is Engaged 81
Our Father is a Defender 85
Our Father is Righteous 89
Our Father is Strong 93
Our Father is Present 97
Our Father is Wise 101
Our Father is Peaceful 105
Our Father is Knowledgeable 109
Our Father is a Leader 113

Our Father Is Light	117
Our Father is Patient	121
The Next Step on the Path	125
The Final Assignment	127

Foreword

When I survey the world with its ever-changing ideas and shifting perspectives, I recognize that we need a guide, a beacon of wisdom that can shape our worldview—the Bible. The worldview it generates offers clarity amidst turmoil, guidance amidst doubt, and purpose amidst aimlessness.

As I consider the Bible's relevance in forming and reshaping our knowledge of the universe and life itself, one component that sticks out is its function in shaping men to be dads. We live in a time when the biblical idea of masculinity is frequently skewed, and the responsibilities of fatherhood are misunderstood; the Bible provides a timeless road map for men to navigate the path of parenthood with grace, strength, and knowledge.

The Bible presents God, our creator, as the archetype for all fathers. The book of Genesis depicts God's love for His children in the act of creation, as well as His desire for companionship through His interaction with Adam and Eve. In Exodus, we find that the Father's core characteristics are mercy, grace, slowness to anger, and abounding and loyal love.

These characteristics find their ultimate manifestation in Jesus Christ. In Christ, the scriptures unveil what love truly is. Love is the choice to humbly lay down one's desires and prerogatives for the sake of bettering another. Jesus laid down His divine rights for us. He humbled himself, joining with humanity to serve us and ultimately die for us so that we could inherit the life of the age to come. If fathers truly want to parent rightly, look at what the father did through Jesus.

In addition to seeing Jesus as our prime example, the Bible contains practical advice on the art of parenting. The book of Proverbs, for example, contains wise instructions on disciplining and instructing children, instilling in them a reverence for God and respect for others. New Testament passages enlighten the path of parenthood by emphasizing crucial truths and faithful applications.

Anthony Vandagriff spends time drawing from the scriptures various attributes and qualities attributed to God, encouraging dads to read, wrestle, and internalize them. Doing so will profoundly impact your life, inviting you to more faithfully reflect the father of all fathers, thus changing not only your life but the lives of your children.

May the wisdom presented in this devotional guide you and empower you to be the fathers God has called you to be and the fathers our world so sorely needs.

In Christ,
Derrick Weeks

A Path for Imperfect Dads

In the world we find ourselves in, nonbelievers and believers often share this idea that God should make everything in life perfect. For the nonbeliever, they might claim God cannot exist because of all the bad that happens, as if to imply that if God did exist, everything would be perfect. Believers sometimes fall into the prosperity, it is mine if I claim it now, camp and believe that only favor and blessings should come their way.

The idea that we gain perfection in this life because of God is not a biblical premise. His work is perfect. His daily sustaining grace is perfect. We, however, are not. So, it is important for us, as dads, to remember, that being a Christian does not make us the perfect dad. Any honest father of faith would admit this to be the case.

None of us are perfect dads and none of us ever will be. Fortunately, that is not our goal. But therein lies the problem. So many dads do not truly understand what it means to be a dad. Some grew up without a father as an example. Some grew up with a father who was a bad example. Many grew up never being taught what it means to be a dad.

In my experience, this was never prioritized. One would think the churches would have focused on this, but I never heard anything about it. My understanding was that it was a natural part of life and if countless men did it before me, I would be able to do it too. Except, I was not sure what I was doing.

I have been blessed to learn some things on my fatherhood journey. One of the greatest revelations was that being a dad is not merely a role I occupy. Fatherhood is not a job we get to retire from once the kids move out of the house. Being a dad is not what we do but rather who we are. It is so much more than a task; it is a change in our identity. We evolve when we become fathers, but we step into an identity we often know little about.

While many of us have men in our lives we can look to, when it comes to understanding who we are and who we are supposed to be as a dad, we need to set our sights on our heavenly Father. He is the one we should emulate and follow. God has perfectly portrayed who a father is and what a father does. In order for us to be who God intends for us to be as dads, we must look to Him and follow His example.

In an attempt to help you with this, I have pulled together thirty attributes of our Father from the scriptures. As you can probably tell from the size of this book, you are not getting an in-depth exegesis of each verse or text. Instead, I have focused on a quality of our Father for each of the thirty devotionals and written a letter to you. These are intended to put a pause in your day and cause you to reflect on God and His attributes so you can determine how to develop those same attributes in your life. As you contemplate these things, I believe you will begin to gain a clearer understanding of your identity as a dad.

My prayer and hope for you is that you will see who God wants you to be as a dad by fixing your eyes on him. That you will learn how to father your children by seeing how your heavenly Father deals with you. That the questions, doubts, and concerns you carry as a dad will be resolved as the scriptures bring clarity on your identity.

I want to help you on the journey of following our Father.

How to Use this Devotional

The concept of a devotional is rooted in the verb, devote, which means to lend all or large portions of your time to something. If you want this to benefit you, take your time. Speed reading through this in a single day will not help you. You need to dwell on each quality of our Father so that you can develop a deeper understanding of your identity as a dad.

Maybe you navigate through this in a month, reading one devotional a day. Maybe you want to take two or three days per topic. Maybe you get four days into it and feel you need to start over. As long as you are committing your time to understanding God as our Father and how his identity helps you better understand your identity as a dad, you are doing it right. Just commit to going through it.

Here is my recommendation. Start out by taking a moment to pray. Thank God for the opportunity this day brings. Thank him for faithfully being present with you. Thank him for the privilege of being a dad and ask him to help you become more like him.

Next, start reading. I recommend reading aloud if you are able to. It allows you to observe the words, think about the words, and hear the words. Regardless, just take your time.

After you have finished reading, jot down any initial thoughts you have in the notes section. Then take time to contemplate and plan how you can fulfill the action item. Do not be afraid to use your notes or reminders app on your phone. After that, if anything else has come to your mind, write it down in the notes section. Finalize your time with prayer, however you see fit.

There is no perfect way to go through a devotional. As long as you are committed to finishing, taking the time you require, seeking to learn and grow, and being honest with yourself, you are doing it right.

Our Father is Love

1 John 4:16 (NIV) - And so we know and rely on the love God has for us. God is love. Whoever lives in love lives in God, and God in them.

There are a lot of things we learn about God when we read the Bible. God is described in so many different ways. We read that God is holy, unique from everything because he alone is the creator. We read that God is strong, mighty, and all-powerful. We read about God's wisdom and all-encompassing knowledge. The psalmist, in Psalm 145, tells us that God is great, and that we cannot even begin the quest to discover just how great God is.

The list of attributes used to describe God is lengthy and the epitome of impressive. Yet, in spite of all of these previous descriptions, John had a different perspective. John was loved by Jesus. John may have been the closest to Jesus of all the disciples. Undoubtedly reflecting on the scriptures and his time with God made manifest, John does not choose to describe God as strong, all-knowing, majestic, or in some other way that we might view as awesome. John considers all of that and writes, "God is love."

As men, we are attracted and drawn to awesomeness. We want to rise to the top. We want to be number one. We want to be the strongest, the smartest, the most liked, the funniest, and whatever else there is a first-place position for. Especially when it comes to our kids, we really want them to think the world of us.

Personally, I love that my kids thought I had mind powers when they were little. I love that my son always wanted to exercise so he could be strong like me. I love that my kids saw these attributes I possessed and thought I was cool because of them. But after seeing John describe God as love with all the other descriptions on the table, I had a change of heart.

I want to encourage you to change your thinking when it comes to what you want your kids to think of when they think about you. Because for us, strength, sharpness, and appearance may all fade, but love stands the test of time.

Approach today with a mindset of "how can I show my kids I love them?" and strive to be a strong, smart, successful, and funny dad who is best described as a dad who loves.

Your Fellow Father,
Anthony

Today's Step:

I want you to make a commitment today that as long as your kid(s) are in your house, there will never be a day that passes where hugs, kisses, affection, and the phrase "I love you," do not come from you. Do not be discouraged to set a reminder on your phone to prompt you to show affection to your kid(s) if you need to. Do whatever you need to do to ensure that your love is obvious to your children every day.

Notes

Our Father is Forgiving

Psalm 86:5 (NIV) - You, Lord, are forgiving and good, abounding in love to all who call to you.

I want you to recall the feelings you had when someone wronged you. You probably felt hurt, betrayed, unappreciated, and the lingering thoughts of "why would they?" and "how could they?" would not seem to go away. There is a good chance you needed an explanation or an apology before you would ever consider reconciling with that person too.

Imagine how God felt. Out of His goodness, He made Adam and Eve, His children. He gave them paradise with one restriction. Still, they chose not to trust him, they disobeyed, they hid from him, and they could not have a straightforward conversation with him. God did nothing wrong. God did nothing to make them untrusting, he gave them no reason to feel like they needed to hide from him, and no reason to feel like they could not talk to him. Yet, that is what they did.

God could have retaliated righteously with justifiable actions. And even though consequences were issued, forgiveness was already present.

In Romans 5, we learn that forgiveness was made available while we were still ungodly and sinners. God did not wait for us to get good enough. Nor did he wait for an apology or explanation for our actions. He forgave us despite it all.

Jesus reveals this quality about himself in Luke 15 with the story of the father of the prodigal son. The son was still a great distance from the house when the father ran out to restore him. The son tried to apologize but his father did not allow him to finish the apology.

Our Father is forgiving, and his forgiveness is ready for us the moment we mess up and need it. He does not think we will learn a lesson by withholding his mercy from us. God forgives quickly.

We sometimes feel we need cause and reason to forgive our kids. They do wrong in a situation or against us and we choose to hold them in this makeshift purgatory where they must await our forgiveness.

Do not forget the debt you were forgiven of. Do not be like the servant who was forgiven of a great debt yet could not forgive the lesser debt owed to him.

If your kid has done something that hurt you or offended you, make today the day you forgive them. The longer you hold on to what happened in the past, the more resentment and bitterness roots in your life.

If you have nothing to forgive in this moment, store up forgiveness now. There will be a day your kid offends you, betrays you, or hurts you. When that day comes, run to them with forgiveness just as God ran to you.

Your Fellow Father,
Anthony

Today's Step:

If your kid has offended you in some way and you have held on to that, today is the day you let go. Today is the day you go to or call that child, and tell them you are sorry, and that they are forgiven.

Notes

Our Father is Gracious

Romans 5:8 (NIV) - But God demonstrates his own love for us in this: While we were still sinners, Christ died for us.

Grace is one of the greatest gifts God gives us and it is one of the greatest gifts we can give our children. Grace is unmerited or undeserved favor. When you have fallen short and done nothing to qualify yourself as deserving, grace still deems you worthy and still blesses you. It truly is amazing.

Just reading Romans 5:8, makes you pause and think. How incredible is it that God would do something so great for us who were so far from greatness! Then to think that his grace remains sufficient for us throughout the course of our life with all the mistakes that we make. Grace remains and grace sustains. Grace makes it possible for us to have an everlasting relationship with God.

As a dad, relationship with your kids is mandatory if you are to fulfill the mission of fatherhood. If you are going to equip and disciple your kids to be a part of God's mission in a greater capacity than yourself, you must maintain a relationship with them. Because without that connection, your voice is not heard, and your actions are not seen. You have no influence without a relationship.

Have you ever had to listen to someone you did not like or respect give a speech or presentation? Did you listen to what they said? There is a good chance you tuned them out because of your disdain for them. Our kids will do the same with us if we do not nurture our relationship with them, and that requires grace.

You have probably figured out by now that your kids are going to disobey you. They will question your rules and authority and experiment doing what they want to do. The worst thing you can do is to get mad and cut them off. What you need to do is give grace and then provide guidance. Rubbing their wrong in their face only creates shame and guilt and those are weights that crush them. If you want them to live and flourish, you have to give grace.

Consider Luke 15, where Jesus likens himself to the father of the prodigal son. The father was disrespected by his son, essentially wished dead by his son, and suffered a stain on his reputation because of his son. If anyone had reason to lash out and scorn their kid, he did. Instead, he ran to his son, his offender, and tackled him with grace.

I pray you will clearly see your mission as a father and the value of your relationship with your children. Through that lens, I hope you will choose grace over guilt. That you will look for opportunities to give grace and to remind your child that they belong to you and that relationship trumps all failures.

Your Fellow Father,
Anthony

Today's Step:

Your kid will mess up today. Do not respond with guilt. Choose to give grace and guidance and top it off with a hug.

Notes

Our Father is Faithful

Lamentations 3:22-23 (NKJV) - Through the LORD's mercies we are not consumed, Because His compassions fail not. They are new every morning; Great is Your faithfulness.

It is one thing to be great, but it is another thing to be dependably great. God is all of these amazing things, but he is faithfully all of these amazing things. He is unwavering and unchanging.

God's faithfulness is hinged upon his identity. He is not faithful depending upon certain situations and he is not faithful when he needs to be. Our Father is faithful constantly because it is right to be so.

While we can instinctively think of God's faithfulness in stories like those of Joseph and Daniel, I want you to see his faithfulness through a different lens. His faithfulness is not seen in remarkable deliverances but rather in the fact he can always be trusted.

God is so faithful that people were willing to lay down their lives believing that God would show himself to be faithful (Hebrews 11). Job makes a perplexing statement while enduring his storm when he says, "though he slay me, yet will I trust him." Job was willing to trust God even if God thought it best to take Job's life. Trust like that is only founded on a dependability like our Father's.

My prayer for you is that you would be dependable for your kids. That the faithfulness you exude gives your children hope. That you would choose to stay the course, always do what is right, live with integrity, and be about God's business.

I want you to live faithfully and be faithful. I want your kids to observe you and interact with you and know that their dad can always be trusted because he is always so faithful.

Examine your life. Make sure your actions align with your values and be faithful in doing what is right.

Your Fellow Father,
Anthony

Today's Step:

This level of faithfulness requires a discipline that may need to be written down in a routine. Consider your values and craft a routine that is in alignment with your values. This should include times for prayer, devotion, exercise, family, and whatever else you value. Some items may be daily, and others may occur weekly. You will not get this perfect on your first attempt but faithfully work on it.

Notes

Our Father is Just

Deuteronomy 32:4 (NLT) - He is the Rock; his deeds are perfect. Everything he does is just and fair. He is a faithful God who does no wrong; how just and upright he is!

Just is not a word we use very often today, unless we are referring to something being "just enough" but that is not how the Bible uses "just." While a bar set that low might be exciting to see, we ought to be glad that is not what our Father aims for.

When the Bible talks about God being just, it encompasses a couple of components. It refers to God being righteous, or in right standing. He has not done anything to create turmoil between himself and creation. It also refers to God doing the things that are right, the things that fall on the side of justice. The actions of God are always in alignment with the law, best understood as those things which are good.

I remember playing this game as a kid, and you might have played it as well, but my friends and I would pose questions about God doing certain things. Usually, our questions leaned toward God doing things outside of his word because he is God and it is his word, why can he not do whatever he wants to do, whenever he wants to do it. The truth is, God does not because God is just. His word is good and eternal, so he eternally honors what is good.

Now if you are thinking perfection, stop. Perfection should never cross your mind because it is unattainable. What you should be thinking about are things in the Bible and things you have spoken, especially to your kids. You cannot talk about how important God is and then prioritize something else above God. You cannot tell your kids you are going to do something and then flake because it is inconvenient.

I mess up at this. You will mess up at this. Still, we need to strive to be just. We need to aim to do the things that are right and good, and to stay in right standing with our children. One thing that will help us ensure we do the right things in front of our children is by making sure we do the right things even when they are not around.

I have had my struggles, and I am sure you have had yours. Being just is choosing to do what is good even when no one will find out about what you do and even when it seems like this choice will not impact anyone. As you go through your day, keep thinking about "is this right?" or "what is the right thing to do?" because you are never wrong to do what is right.

Your Fellow Father,
Anthony

Today's Step:

Think about what you do to pass time and determine if those things would be considered just. Make a list of things you could do instead. Things that strengthen your relationship with God, your wife, or your kids. You can try to find a new park or place to take your kids. You can try to learn a new language in preparation for that trip your wife really wants to take. If the things you choose to do serve God, your wife, and your kids, they are just.

Notes

Our Father is Creative

Genesis 1:1 (NIV) - In the beginning God created the heavens and the earth.

While the Bible tells us that all things were created by him and for him, God also intended his creation for us. Adam was given dominion to rule and take care of God's creation; to be a part of what God was doing. God created wondrous things to share with us.

Today I want you to take a moment to just look at the sky. I want you to see the variation in colors, design, and texture. As you study it, you will be overcome with marvel and that marvel will cause you to think about God and how good he is.

This is because the heavens declare his glory; his goodness. We can look in the Genesis account and confirm that as everything was created, it was analyzed and deemed good. When we look at what God has created, we get a fresh reminder of him and of how wonderful he is.

Maybe you do not consider yourself to be the artsy or creative type; that is not mandatory for this. You have the capacity to create a number of things for your children. You can utilize your artistic side, your construction prowess, your financial knowledge, and even your organizational capabilities.

Maybe you paint a masterpiece, maybe you build a stepstool like I did for my oldest daughter, maybe you put together a fund that will be a tremendous blessing for your child when they graduate high school, or maybe you just plan the best trips or activities at the house.

The main point is that you are intentional about creating things that can be shared with your children. The things that you create should cause your children to remember you and to remember just how much you love them. So today, take time to reflect on your strengths and think about what you could create for your kids. Again, it can be an experience, or it can be something material that will last. We are to be creative and that means we create throughout this life.

There will be things that you organize and create for your kids that they will not appreciate as much as you wanted them to. That is normal. Just keep creating.

Your Fellow Father,
Anthony

Today's Step:

You might not have time today to start and finish your creation, but you can start planning. Jot down some ideas and create a plan. Remember everything does not have to be extravagant, small moments are things you can create too.

Notes

Our Father is a Provider

Philippians 4:19 (NIV) - And my God will meet all your needs according to the riches of his glory in Christ Jesus.

This is a quality that many men in our culture immediately correlate with being a dad. However, it is often narrowed down to money and material needs. Dads feel they need to provide money, food, shelter, and clothing. That about sums it up.

I am not opposing that. I strive to provide those things myself and I encourage you to do the same. It might be a good idea for us to check ourselves when it comes to being providers though. What we do not want to do is be as the Pharisees were when Jesus told them they fixated on the visible, exterior things and not the vital, inner components.

Consider our Father and the ways he provides. Yes, he owns the cattle of a thousand hills and does bless us financially, but as Paul writes to the church at Philippi, God meets or provides for all needs.

The apostle Paul speaks of a thorn in his side that troubled him. He writes that he prayed three times for something to be done, likely desiring the problem to be taken care of. God, though, provided what Paul really needed. He gave him all-sufficient grace to overcome and to move forward.

Thomas, overwhelmed with grief and anguish after losing his leader, the one he wholeheartedly believed would bring hope and salvation, was unable to believe Christ had risen. At a time when his faith was failing, God provided proof.

Being a provider for your kids requires a lot more than a job, money, and material assets. There will be moments when the shoulder you lend your child to cry on and the hand you extend for them to hold on to will be of greater value than the trip you spend thousands of dollars on.

So today, look and listen, and learn what your kid needs. You providing what you think they need is not the same as what they truly need.

Keep working for those things that are external but be more diligent about their needs that are unseen.

Your Fellow Father,
Anthony

Today's Step:

Pay attention to your kid(s) today and look for their needs, the ones that are not solved by money. Maybe they need your support, a hug, a talk, or more of your time. Aim to provide what they truly need today.

Notes

Our Father is a Teacher

Psalm 32:8 (NIV) - I will instruct you and teach you in the way you should go; I will counsel you with my loving eye on you.

Sometimes when we think about a teacher, we focus on the lectures and the verbal lessons that are delivered in class. There are plenty of those but there is something else good teachers do; they get involved beyond the words. I was fortunate to have teachers who would show us examples of how to complete the task at hand and teachers who would take extra time with me if I needed it. Good teachers do not just explain something once and then sit and wait for you to finish the assignment. Good teachers work with you to help you learn.

Our Father is the greatest teacher because he got involved. God became like us so that we could see, touch, and better understand his lessons. Jesus walked next to his followers, mingled with the people, and spoke in ways they could understand. Jesus illustrated lessons with his actions so his disciples, his students, could watch and learn. He accepted questions and provided explanations and insight. God did not require that we rose to a particular place before he could teach us. God met us where we were in order to teach and show us how to follow him.

There is a good chance you have lived your life striving to climb some ladder. Maybe you have chased wealth and financial status. Maybe you have pursued corporate status and position. Maybe you have attempted to grow as an influencer on a particular subject matter. There is a good chance you have spent your days trying to elevate who you are. But if you want to be a teacher, like our

Father, you have to learn to step down from your status and onto your child's level.

Your child cannot bridge the gap from where they are to where they see you, and remember, they see you a lot better than you actually are. You have to guide them and teach them by getting down to where they are and instructing them on the next steps. You will not effectively teach your child from your self-proclaimed throne. You will effectively teach them by sitting on the floor where they enjoy playing.

If you have younger kids, spend more time on the floor. If you have kids that like to be outside, be outside with them. If they are driving, spend more time in the passenger seat. You need to be intentional about being where your children are because that is the place you will be able to teach them best.

Pride will teach them how far they are from you. Humility will teach them how much farther they can go.

Your Fellow Father,
Anthony

Today's Step:

Get on your kid's level whether it be the floor, outside, with a controller in hand, or in the passenger seat. Within that environment aim to teach something small but at least meet them where they are.

Notes

Our Father is a Communicator

John 10:27 (NLT) - My sheep listen to my voice; I know them, and they follow me.

Communication is a mandatory component of relationships. In short, communication builds trust and trust provides a foundation for a relationship to be built. Additionally, communication continues to nurture and grow that relationship. Understanding that, it makes sense that we find God being an avid communicator with people throughout the Bible.

From the beginning we see God had a routine with Adam and Eve where he would walk and talk with them in the garden. God continually talked to his people through leaders and prophets to provide guidance, instruction, and correction. When Jesus steps onto the scene, it makes perfect sense that we find him constantly talking to people.

We also see that God listens. He listened to Adam and Eve. He listened to Abraham regarding Sodom and Gomorrah. He listened to the prayers and requests made by his people, and he responded. Communication is not just about talking to someone. Communication is also about listening. If God, who has all knowledge, listens to us instead of just telling us exactly what he wants us to do, we must do the same.

You need to establish a lifestyle of communication with your kids. They need to know when they speak to you that you are listening and speaking to help them. The trust developed in that setting will prompt them to come to you whenever issues or questions arise, and that is exactly what you should want.

You also need to initiate conversation early on. Our Father does not sit around on his throne waiting to be contacted by his children. He initiates conversation because he is genuinely interested in us. So, speak to your kids in the morning, if you get to pick them up from school, at the dinner table, and when you are driving around with them.

Please do not jeopardize your relationship with your kids because you do not know what to say or talk about. You have lived a life, and you have stories. Your kids will love your stories. It is refreshing for your kids to hear you are human and that you made mistakes. Just start talking.

But please make sure you listen to your kids because if they do not feel heard by you, they will seek someone else. They may not always need your ability to solve every problem in two sentences. They may just need you to listen and acknowledge that you hear them. Just remember, in order for you to say the right thing, you need to hear what they need.

Your Fellow Father,
Anthony

Today's Step:

Ask your kid(s) how they felt about today. You can get specific and ask if anything made them happy or sad. Try to extract an emotion and then share a story of when you had a similar feeling. By doing this you deepen your connection with your children and model for them what it looks like to trust someone in conversation.

Notes

Our Father is Unchanging

Malachi 3:6 (ESV) - For I the LORD do not change; therefore you, O children of Jacob, are not consumed.

It is amazing how God is unchanging. What and who he was, is true today, and guaranteed tomorrow. We can rely on that. We do not have to fret that his grace may not be sufficient for us when we wake up tomorrow because our Father is unchanging.

This attribute of consistency grants us something eternal, hope. Because we know that God is always with us, we can have hope walking through the darkest valley. We can navigate difficult times of hopelessness with hope because we know God can perform miracles today just as he did back then. Because God is forever the same and unchanging, we can have everlasting hope.

I want you to be unchanging as you continually change. (You might need to read that again)

Being the dad your children need you to be requires growth, but growth requires change. You will change the way you think about things. You will change some of your habits and disciplines. You will change throughout the years, but you can still be unchanging.

You might come to believe your physical health is more important than you have realized, and you might begin to prioritize exercise. You can make that change and still be consistent about making time with your family. There will be several things that change for you but there must be some constants:

Your devotion to God

Your commitment to your marriage
Your love and intentionality toward your children

If ever a change jeopardizes any of these three, you need to think diligently about whether or not that change is worth it. Your children need to be able to depend on you being who you have always been. They need hope for all of the challenges that they will face. They need to know; dad will be there for them.

As you prepare to embark on this day, consider your recent actions. Have you allowed change that has pulled you further from God? Have you felt distant from your wife? Can you recall a recent memory you created with your children? If these relationships seem weaker, please address the changes you have made.

I want you to seek to grow but please be diligent and disciplined in your devotion to Christ, to your wife, and to your children. I pray these three elements will forever be unchanging in your life and that your consistency will offer a lasting hope to your children.

Your Fellow Father,
Anthony

Today's Step:

Take time to think about your typical week in comparison with the values: God, marriage, and children. Is there anything out of place that clashes with these values or that supersedes any of these values? Identify these issues and work to eliminate them.

Notes

Our Father is Proactive

Revelation 3:20 (NIV) - Here I am! I stand at the door and knock. If anyone hears my voice and opens the door, I will come in and eat with that person, and they with me.

This is one of the most incredible attributes of God in my opinion. It is difficult to comprehend and simultaneously humbling, that God would proactively seek and pursue me. Once I saw this in the Bible, I could not stop seeing it.

In Genesis 3:15, following the fall, God let Adam and Eve know that redemption was coming for them. All throughout Isaiah we read that God had a plan, by his own arm, to bring redemption to his people. We get to the New Testament and see that the Father seeks us (implying action) in John 4. In our opening scripture, God tells us that he comes to our house, stands at our door, and keeps on knocking.

It is amazing to me that God did not sit around and wait for me to get things together or to meet some qualifying standard. Instead, he proactively pursued me with love, grace, and redeeming mercy.

Seeing this makes me realize just how much God loves me and I wholeheartedly believe that emulating this for our children will allow them to see just how much we love them.

Start with the little things that you can do first. You can aim to greet your kids first in the morning. You can take care of something the night before so that they do not have to worry about it the next day. You can initiate the hug. You can even (and should) be the first one to apologize if there is a dispute.

These proactive steps lead you toward a closer relationship with your kids. Just as God went to extreme lengths to bring us back in relationship with him, you need to determine what you can be proactive about to nurture the relationship you have with your children.

Part of leading is going first. Be the dad who is genuinely interested in your children, who seeks conversations with them, who asks them to help you, who asks them to take a trip with you simply to run errands, and who first inquires how things are going in their life.

They cannot follow you if you are not taking the first steps. Be proactive.

Your Fellow Father,
Anthony

Today's Step:

Today, initiate the hug and the "I love you." If your kids are grown and out of the house, call them and let them know you love them. Make a habit of this.

Notes

Our Father is Everlasting

Isaiah 9:6 (NIV) - For to us a child is born, to us a son is given, and the government will be on his shoulders. And he will be called Wonderful Counselor, Mighty God, Everlasting Father, Prince of Peace.

If the title gave you the impression that I was going to tell you where to find the Holy Grail so you could obtain immortality, you are out of luck. This is a devotional with no connection to Indiana Jones. But while there will come a day you will pass from this earth; you can still be an everlasting dad.

The prophet Isaiah crafts our key verse within a particular context. He is making references to kings who came after Uzziah, who ruled selfishly with no care for God's purpose. Isaiah was contrasting the coming Messiah and setting him above those kings. One way he did this was by identifying him as the everlasting Father.

Jesus is depicted this way because he would be fatherly to his children throughout time. Unlike other kings and rulers who flaked or eventually died, Jesus would timelessly be an everlasting father. It was a promise and commitment to be a father regardless of circumstance.

What I want you to take away from this is the identity factor. This was not a role to be temporarily filled, but an identity to be eternally embraced. That is true for us too.

You are not simply trying to get a job done by raising kids with retirement coming once you are empty nesting. You have been given a new identity by God that is purpose-filled and eternal.

As a dad, you are making disciples. You are leading, loving, and investing in your kids. You will certainly be more hands on when they are younger, but even after they become mature adults with families of their own, you are still called to be there, to be the dad they need. Realize and embrace your everlasting identity of dad.

Your Fellow Father,
Anthony

Today's Step:

While it can take time to make the mental shift that being a dad is not simply something you do, but rather who you have become, you can make an expression that affirms this truth. At some point today, say this to your kid(s), "I am so glad that I am and will always be blessed to be your dad, because (fill in the blank)." Make sure you get specific. Your children are too important for generic sentiments.

Notes

Our Father is Committed

Deuteronomy 7:9 (NLT) - Understand, therefore, that the LORD your God is indeed God. He is the faithful God who keeps his covenant for a thousand generations and lavishes his unfailing love on those who love him and obey his commands.

Commitment is a beautiful thing. There is such a comfort and reassurance we have with those who have committed themselves to us. We can rely on them, always.

God has committed himself to us and we see that in the scriptures. Our Father made eternal promises to always be our God, among other things, and to stay in relationship with us. He honored this commitment even when others did not.

God had plenty of opportunity to rightfully forsake his creation, but he did not because he made a commitment. He carried this out to the extreme by bearing the weight of the cross while we still basked in our sins. Our Father honored his commitment.

This shows us something important about commitment, which is, commitment is not deterred by exterior elements such as others or our feelings.

You have made a commitment to God and to your children, to bring your kids up in the training and instruction of the Lord. There is nothing your kids can do that should push you to stray from that mission. You should always be a godly example whose speech is centered around scripture. Even if your kids decide they do not want to serve Christ for a season. You do not give up and break your commitment because of them. It is your commitment to keep.

Secondly, I know there are bad days. Those days can often stir up feelings that encourage us to give up or indulge in past behaviors. Your commitment should not be swayed by your feelings. That can make commitments challenging but the things that are challenging in life are often the things worth doing.

You have commitments to God, your wife, your kids, and others. Do not allow something like a disagreement with your wife to make you flake on your commitment to her. Do not allow a challenging day to make you step away from the things you have committed to do.

You have made your commitments for a reason. Stay the course.

Your Fellow Father,
Anthony

Today's Step:

Your commitment to your family should be rooted in your commitment to God. Set reminders for Bible reading and prayer if you are inconsistent in these areas. Also, reach out to a friend and see if once a month you can chat about what you have read in the Bible. These reminders will soon become habits and disciplines, and ultimately delights.

Notes

Our Father is Honest

Titus 1:2 (NLT) - This truth gives them confidence that they have eternal life, which God--who does not lie--promised them before the world began.

Can you imagine a world without lying? On the one hand, it would be great to know you were always receiving information you could depend on. On the other hand, it could be dangerous when your wife wants to know how that dress makes her look.

All humor aside, it is refreshing to know God always speaks the truth, even when it is not what we want to hear or when it hurts. But it is also assuring to know God is always honest in his actions. God always does what he says he will do, and God always does good.

I want you to be a man of your word. I want you to speak truth. If you are not honest, you will never have trust, and without trust you will never have a strong relationship. But even more than that, I want you to be honest in the things that you do.

Even with a family, you have private time. It may seem like your kids follow you everywhere, but you still have time to yourself. What do you do with that time? Do you commit it to your personal development? Do you use it for the benefit of your wife or children? Or is there something below the surface that you keep hidden?

We live in a visual world, and you likely have multiple devices you could use to access things you do not need to be looking at. But this applies to more than pornography. Maybe you mindlessly scroll on social media wasting hours of your life that you will never get back. Maybe you gamble. Maybe you abuse particular substances. You can fill in the blank with whatever your particular poison is.

I want you to aspire to be honest like our Father, so I want you to ask something. Would you be ok if your wife and children knew what you did in your private time? If you answer "no" then whatever you are doing in your private time is not ok.

Live honestly. By doing this you constantly build your relationships, and you give your family hope and assurance. Give your family no reason to question you.

If you have things you need to stop doing and that you need to change, do not wait. Make today the day you live honestly. Utilize a friend to help keep you accountable. Be intentional about conversations with people who inspire you to grow. Separate yourself from the things that you struggle with. Your family depends on it. Your influence as a father depends on it.

Remember, if you are not ok with people knowing the things you do in secret, then the things you are doing in secret are not ok.

Your Fellow Father,
Anthony

Today's Step:

Are there things you keep private from your wife and kids because you would be ashamed or embarrassed if they knew about them? It is time to eliminate those things. Reach out to a friend who can help you be accountable. If you are low on friends, send an email to fatheringourfuture@gmail.com.

Notes

Our Father is a Servant

Mark 10:45 (NIV) - For even the Son of Man did not come to be served, but to serve, and to give his life as a ransom for many.

I am not sure being a servant is a choice most people would make. I would be more inclined to think that you would rather have a servant than be one yourself. Maybe that would change depending on who you would be serving. If it is someone you value and look up to, you could potentially learn some great things.

That is the bizarre thing about God's decision to be a servant. There was no one God could idolize to serve. He looked way down to the undeserving, us. Was there a benefit for God in doing this? On the surface level, no. Our Father chose to become a servant because he loved us, and it was an opportunity to be close to us.

The other component of God's servanthood that is wild to me is referenced in Philippians 2. Paul wrote that Christ cast aside his reputation and became a servant. This runs parallel with the father of the prodigal in Luke 15. The father ran out to greet his son. That was the responsibility of the servants and running was not something someone of his age and status would have done. But the father set aside reputation and became a servant to be close to his son.

I know it can be a challenge. The old school method that most of us saw was the child serving the parent. We are bigger, smarter, and stronger. We deserve the respect and reverence. But how much more does God? If he serves us, we have no excuse.

Seek opportunities to serve your kids. Find ways you can help them. I am not saying do everything for them and keep them from responsibilities. I want you to serve them in ways that teach them lessons.

Let your service to them provide guidance on how to treat others. Allow your service to them to make grace more tangible for them. Help them see the value of loving others through how you serve them.

Lastly, I want you to ask yourself if you would be willing to give up your reputation for them. Do you esteem your children above the image others make of you? Do not allow yourself to be infatuated with your personal image, wealth, or career more so than your value of your children.

Take a step down from your perch, kneel down to their feet, and find ways to serve them.

Your Fellow Father,
Anthony

Today's Step:

How can you serve your kid(s) today? If they are young, maybe you assist or take over one of their chores for today. If they are older, maybe you fill up their car with gas or treat them to lunch. Do not be afraid to ask them, "How can I serve you or help you today?"

Notes

Our Father is an Example

1 Peter 2:21 (NLT) - For God called you to do good, even if it means suffering, just as Christ suffered for you. He is your example, and you must follow in his steps.

God is the epitome of an example. An example takes the abstract and makes it tangible. For example, (pun intended) I could talk to you about love, what it is, and what it does and say, "For example, 1 Corinthians 13." By giving an example, I provide you with a context to use when thinking about the abstract. Using 1 Corinthians 13 would help you understand love properly, instead of confusing it with cultural movements that dilute its true meaning. An example helps you see the unseen.

This is exactly what God did for us. God spoke his ways, will, and instructions but then that spoken word became flesh. Jesus was the visible of the invisible. Jesus told others when they looked at him, they were seeing the Father. God became like us, modeled his precepts, and paved a path for us to follow.

As fathers, we possess the same opportunity. We do not need to function as a coach for our kids, where we simply tell them what to do. We cannot sit around on the couch demanding that our kids are up and moving around. When we do those things, we are being an example, but not a good one. We are showing them a dysfunctional authority. We are displaying a bad image of what it is to be an adult or a parent.

I want you to rise to the occasion and be an example to your children like our Father has been for us. Their eyes are on you constantly. Let them see what patience looks like when things get chaotic. Let them see what grace looks like when they fail. Let them see what love looks like when it is not determined by accomplishments. Let them see what it looks like to trust God when situations are beyond your control.

Your kids may remember certain phrases from you, but what they see from you will stick with them forever. Your behavior, mannerisms, and actions leave an eternal impression on their hearts and minds. This happens whether you are mindful of it or not. So please, be mindful of the things that you do. Strive to live out godly principles. Aim to exercise a lifestyle yielded to the leading of God's Spirit.

Do this so that when your kids look at you, they actually see more of God.

Your Fellow Father,
Anthony

Today's Step:

Take your kid with you for an errand or have them join you in whatever it is you are doing so that they can see you in action. Explain to them what you are doing and why it is important or necessary. There are lessons and examples in just about everything that you do. Bring your kid along, so they can see.

Notes

Our Father is a Comforter

2 Corinthians 1:3-4 (NIV) - Praise be to the God and Father of our Lord Jesus Christ, the Father of compassion and the God of all comfort, who comforts us in all our troubles, so that we can comfort those in any trouble with the comfort we ourselves receive from God.

Our Father has the power and capability to solve all our problems for us, but he does not. While this is something that sometimes bothers us, it should make a lot of sense to us.

We know, as dads, if we step into every conflict and challenge our child has, and solve everything for them, we handicap them. They never develop the ability to function on their own and they typically become spoiled. So even though God has the power to solve our issues, God does not want to spoil us.

What our Father does, instead of doing everything for us, is he comforts us. As we endure challenging obstacles or situations, he is there, not always propelling us through but comforting us as we go.

When the Bible speaks of God comforting us, it can mean a few things. It can mean to strengthen, encourage, teach, and to call to one's side. God comforts us through our struggles by calling us to come to him, to be where he is. It is in that place that our Father edifies and encourages us for the path ahead. It is in that place that our Father provides instruction for how we can navigate the challenges we are facing. This is how God comforts us.

So as dads, we need to look and pay close attention to our kids. When we see they are struggling, we do not always need to step in and fix everything for them, even though we may be inclined to do that instinctively. Instead, we need to call them to our side and remind them that they are not alone in this.

My prayer and desire for you is to be a comforter for your children. To be a father who looks for opportunities to teach and instruct your children on how to navigate the struggles in front of them. To be a dad who affirms your children. Who speaks life and encouragement to them that morphs into strength.

As a comforter, you're not conquering all of their conflicts, but you are assuring them that you'll be with them, cheering for them, as they grow through their journeys.

Your Fellow Father,
Anthony

Today's Step:

I want you to have a conversation with your kid(s) today. Ask them how they feel presently in life. Do not seek to solve anything, just listen. Toward the end of the conversation, I want you to let your child know that you are there for them and that they can come to you whenever they feel they need to.

Notes

Our Father is Selfless

John 15:13 (NKJV) - Greater love has no one than this, than to lay down one's life for his friends.

Imagine you have all power, all knowledge, and the ability to do anything you want when you want. What would you do?

I will tell you what God did. God gave himself for us. God's desire for us was so great that he chose to serve us over himself.

Did God need us? Probably not. Would God be just fine without us? Likely so. But God loved us and because he loved us, he gave. Because that is what love does. As the Apostle Paul writes in 1 Corinthians 13, "Love is not self-seeking."

This is why when we read the Bible, we find God constantly working on our behalf and serving his creation. Our Father's affection is toward us and so he selflessly looks to help us.

I want you to think about your relationship with your family. Do you put them first, or do they come after you have done what you want to do? Are you unwilling to change your lifestyle and to let go of certain hobbies so that you can more greatly serve them? I want to caution you that if you choose yourself, then you will lose them.

God models how we should love and live, in addition to scripture that instructs us how to love and live, such as Ephesians 5:25. If God chose this path of selflessness in his infinite wisdom, why would we question that in our ignorance?

Take the father in Luke 15. He would have been justified in rejecting his son who tarnished his reputation and wasted his fortunes. It would have made more sense for him to protect his legacy by not giving this foolish son access to his riches again. But this father was not living for himself. This father was living for his children. So, there was no second thought about waiting and watching for his son. There was no second guessing running out to meet him like a servant would do. There was no doubt in his mind that he should reinstate his son fully. Because love gives, not for selfish gain, but for the benefit of others.

There may be some things in your life that you prioritize because you want those things. I want you to take a deep look inwardly and determine if you are living selfishly. If there are changes to make, start making them. Because love does not gain for yourself, love gives for others.

Your Fellow Father,
Anthony

Today's Step:

Consider your schedule, habits, and hobbies. Are there things you are holding on to that negatively impact your ability to serve your family? If so, it is time to let go.

Notes

Our Father is Principled

Psalm 138:2 (NLT) - I bow before your holy Temple as I worship. I praise your name for your unfailing love and faithfulness; for your promises are backed by all the honor of your name.

We have all heard talk about, and likely personally aimed at, being a man of principles. Living our lives in such a way where others know where we stand because rules or a code dictate how we conduct ourselves. Our Father functions like this.

Psalm 138:2 tells us that God has backed his word by his name. His name that is above all names, that, on one day, every knee will bow to. His word is esteemed and honored according to the greatness of his name. This level of honor and reverence for his word is seen in how God conducts himself. God does not lie and so God holds himself to the standard of what he speaks.

The word declares God will never leave us or forsake us, and so God eternally binds himself to that. God spoke to Adam and Eve that their seed would one day crush the head of the serpent and that was carried out thousands of years later by Christ. When God speaks, he always honors and stays true to his word.

Do you strive to live this way? Not only in honoring your own word but more so in faithfully living by God's word. Can others look at what you do and know clearly what guides your life as James speaks about in his epistle? Are you a man of principles?

My desire for you is that you would take to heart the words God spoke to Joshua. The Lord instructed Joshua to meditate on the word day and night so that he would be careful to do, or live by, all that was written.

Be in God's word more than the words of anyone or anything else. No human will ever give you greater words to live by than Jesus Christ. No email will ever give you content more relevant than the scriptures. Let the principles laid out by our Father be the principles you allow to guide your life.

Your Fellow Father,
Anthony

Today's Step:

You know how you operate. If you immediately check your email in the mornings, subscribe to a newsletter that sends you a scripture each day. Download a Bible app onto your phone and allow it to send you a notification where you are alerted about the scripture of the day. Set a reminder on your mobile device that prompts you to read the Bible. You need to be in the word, and you need to stay in the word.

Notes

Our Father is Engaged

Matthew 10:30 (ESV) - But even the hairs of your head are all numbered.

Do not worry, no bald jokes today.

God made the world we live in down to the most microscopic, fascinating detail. The earth functions with such precision that generation after generation marvels at its complexities. While we get captivated at the functionality of creation, God remains captivated with us.

Our Father genuinely desires a relationship with us and so we see that he does not sit high on his throne, but instead he chooses to be engaged with us.

Historically, we can track God's involvement with his people, from the exodus to the incarnation, and even to this day through the infilling of God's Spirit. Our Father does not just sit around, he engages with us and our lives.

It is a good thing for you to be around when your kids are up and doing their thing, but be encouraged to engage with them. You might get on the floor with them to play there game or you might need to go with them to a place they like to visit. Step out of the exclusive plan you have for yourself and participate in what they are doing.

This helps your child see value in themselves because your engagement allows them to see you value them. If the greatest person in the world, in their eyes, thinks they are valuable, they will start to believe it themselves.

Engagement also equips you to see where they are physically, emotionally, mentally, and spiritually. That knowledge allows you to help them where they are.

There are daily opportunities for you to engage with your children. Please open your eyes and see them. They go deeper than the "how was school?" conversation.

My prayer is that you will not join the company of those who have expressed the regret of not doing enough with their children as they approached their final breath. The opportunity is right in front of you. Be engaged, participate, and be involved in your child's life.

Your Fellow Father,
Anthony

Today's Step:

Whatever you had planned for yourself today, scratch it. Today you are going to ask your kids what they are doing or what they would like to do, and you are going to participate and engage in that activity with them.

Notes

Our Father is a Defender

Psalm 18:2 (NLT) - The LORD is my rock, my fortress, and my savior; my God is my rock, in whom I find protection. He is my shield, the power that saves me, and my place of safety.

I am sure some of my Texan brothers saw the theme for today and gave an affectionate double tap to their side arm. Unfortunately, that is not quite the angle I am taking.

Our God is strong. He is called "the Almighty." Our Father stands as this tower, this mountain that we can run to and find safety and security in. He defends us.

We can look through the Bible and see these remarkable ways God defended his people. The exodus may be the zenith. We watch the children of Israel pass through the Red Sea and then we see God close the waters down on the Egyptian army. As I am writing this there is a side within me saying, "Oh yeah!" because there is desire to dominate, in a similar fashion, people or forces that may come against my children. I do not think that is a bad thing. I believe that is a natural instinct that we are given by God as dads. There is an element of control and wisdom we need to merge with it, but that is for another time.

We also see God defend his people in another way. He defended Mary and Joseph by instructing them where to travel. The Lord, as the shepherd, defends the sheep by protecting them in the valley, but also by guiding them through areas of safety. Our Father defends us when we are in danger and by keeping us from danger.

I believe most of us have the natural inclination to physically rush in to defend our children, so I want to focus on the other aspect of being a defender. What are you building to help keep your children safe and strong? What are you guarding them from in how you raise them? Are you setting up boundaries that grant them true freedom and health physically, mentally, emotionally, and spiritually?

We need to be proactive in defending our kids and not just from physical harm. We need to defend our children from poverty by leading with financial wisdom. We need to defend our children from sexual promiscuity by being brave enough to talk about sex.

This starts with you constructing yourself into a strong tower for them. You cannot defend your children from things you choose to dabble in. Become a place they can run to for security and assurance. Be brave enough to do things for your kids that maybe were not done for you. Be wise enough to look ahead and research so that you can create boundaries for your kids that will help them prosper.

Stay tough, but know defending your kids is not always a reaction. Defending your kids is often a proactive decision.

Your Fellow Father,
Anthony

Today's Step:

You need to become a trusted conversation partner with your kids. You do not achieve this by making them tell you everything, you achieve this by opening up to them about things in your past or that you are currently dealing with to let them know you trust them. You can do this during a car ride, while running an errand, or prior to tucking them into bed.

Create this bond, like the shepherd to the sheep, and you will position yourself to defend them.

Notes

Our Father is Righteous

Psalm 145:17 (NIV) - The LORD is righteous in all his ways and faithful in all he does.

Being righteous is not a common or familiar term in our world today. Most understand it to be something good but that is usually where the understanding stops. A very simple way to comprehend being righteous is to think of it as being in right standing.

When we look at our Father, we can see that he is righteous or in right standing with us and creation as a whole. God never lies. God comes through on every promise made. God consistently does what is best. We cannot look at God and make a justifiable claim that he is not in the right. Our Father is righteous.

As dads, we should take relationships seriously. Righteousness is not simply about doing things that are good, it is about doing things that maintain our right place with others. For example, if you tell your kids to not do something but you constantly do it yourself, you probably are not in right standing with them.

Aiming to be righteous should prompt you to take an inward look at how you function with others. Are you in right standing with God, your wife, your kids, and those you come in contact with? Take time to think about that because if you are anything like me, there is a good chance you are out of place in one of your relationships.

Here is the catch. Your righteousness will never cut it. As Isaiah puts it, in twenty-first century vernacular, our righteous actions are like used tampons. That is quite the visual.

While we may not have it in us, our Father does. And he imputes his righteousness to us as we have faith in him.

My prayer for you today is that you would consider where you stand in the eyes of those you are in relationship with. That after making that reflection, you would seek action for change by embracing your faith in Christ. Decide to be diligent in prayer, in personal devotion to the scriptures, and to community with other disciples.

Desire his righteousness so that you can be in right standing with those you love, serve, and lead.

Your Fellow Father,
Anthony

Today's Step:

Some instances are so obvious that we can determine for ourselves if we are not in right standing with our children. However, I want you to ask your kid(s) if there is anything you have done that has negatively impacted them. Once you know what it is, apologize, make amends, and act to restore your right standing with them.

Notes

Our Father is Strong

Jeremiah 32:17 (NLT) - "O Sovereign LORD! You made the heavens and earth by your strong hand and powerful arm. Nothing is too hard for you!

God has an impressive résumé when it comes to acts of strength. One that astounds me is when Joshua and the children of Israel are in battle, and they pray for God to keep the sun in its place.

Have you ever taken a second to think about that? The sun does not move. The earth rotates and revolves in tandem with the solar system around the sun. God did not stop the sun. God held the universe at a standstill. Absolutely fascinating.

But as fascinating as that may be, that is not the greatest feat of our Father's strength. God showed strength in ways no one even considered.

Think back to Moses preparing to see God in the mountain. The Bible says Moses was going to see God's glory. As it takes place in Exodus 34:6-7, we read not about God's might and strength but about his compassion, grace, and love.

God's glory is not in his power, like we may dream for ourselves, but rather in his love. Our Father was strong enough to do what we could not do for ourselves. He was strong enough to bear the burden we could not. He was strong enough to do it even when it was unappreciated.

In Revelation 5, John writes about a vision where no one was worthy to take the scroll. Then someone declared that the lion of the tribe of Judah had come. John turns to see this mighty force but see something different. He sees a lamb that looked like it had been slain.

I want you to be strong and healthy. I want you to be around as long as you can all while showing your kids that you have still got it. But having strength like our Father looks less like the lion and more like the lamb.

I want you to be strong in how you love, mighty in mercy, and great in grace. Let your strength be seen, not at the gym, but in how hard you are willing to work for and serve your family.

This requires a big mental shift but I know you can do it. Be diligent in prayer, faithful in the word, and mindful of the ways you can love your family.

Your Fellow Father,
Anthony

Today's Step:

Think about and write down one thing, out of the norm, that you can do to serve each person in your home. Now make it happen.

Notes

Our Father is Present

Psalm 139:8 (NLT) - If I go up to heaven, you are there; if I go down to the grave, you are there.

It is comforting and reassuring to know that God is always with us. Our Father will never abandon us or leave us alone. Wherever we go, he is present. Knowing this, we have hope.

Because when he is present in our distress, we can access his peace. When he is present in our trouble, he can protect us. When he is there in our season of famine, he can provide for us. Just as David writes in Psalm 23, there is no reason to fear even in the deepest darkness because God is present.

The thing about being present that we often misunderstand is due to our fixation on location. Too many have interpreted being present as being nearby, next to, or in the same room. While there are benefits we offer our children just by our physical presence, being present entails a little bit more than that.

When we look at God's presence, we see a preparedness. It is not just about God being with us. It is about his ability and commitment to act when he is with us. If I stood next to you while someone beat the snot out of you, that would not be very special. If while I was with you, I was prepared to defend you if someone attacked you and I followed through with that commitment, that would be special. In that instance, my presence would actually mean something.

Your children need to know that your presence means something. They need to have a joy, peace, and comfort when you are close to them because they have a knowledge and faith that your presence actually offers a benefit. None of us want our kids to grow up and offer the sentiment, "Dad was always there, but…"

In order to accomplish this, you will need to prioritize being present physically, but you will also need to pay attention so that you know there needs. Your presence provides nothing if you are not aware of what is lacking. So be present, participate in what they are doing, and be prepared to act.

Lastly, remember that the time you have with your children is continuously a blessing. Time keeps ticking, and life keeps making its demands. It is very easy to lose sight of the wonder in front of you. They change every day and leaving for a moment can mean you miss milestones. Stay present and embrace your blessing.

Your Fellow Father,
Anthony

Today's Step:

Do something with your kid for one hour today and keep your phone away. After you have done that, come back to this devotional, and record how it felt.

Notes

Our Father is Wise

Romans 11:33 (NIV) - Oh, the depth of the riches of the wisdom and knowledge of God! How unsearchable his judgments, and his paths beyond tracing out!

Story after story of God makes it plain to see that our Father is wise. It is one thing to be knowledgeable, or in God's case, to be omniscient, but it is another thing to be wise. Having a wealth of knowledge is wonderful, but knowing how to put that knowledge into action is wisdom.

One story that comes to mind is the story of Joseph in the latter portion of Genesis. Joseph was born into a family with a whole lot of dysfunction and some crazy things happened because of that dysfunction. Case in point, Joseph's brothers attempted to kill him, soon felt remorse, and instead sold him as a slave to strangers (so much better).

As we track through Joseph's life, we see a lot of wild turns and disappointment, but at the end everything comes together. We eventually read this in Genesis 50:20,

"You intended to harm me, but God intended it for good to accomplish what is now being done, the saving of many lives."

God used his wisdom to orchestrate Joseph's life to lead him to a higher purpose. God did not just sit back, knowing all of the tragedy that would befall Joseph, and decide to see how it would play out. He used wisdom to transform misery into meaning.

I want to encourage you to pray for wisdom and look for opportunities to use it. Maybe there are some mistakes you need to be willing for your kid to make instead of attempting to control everything. Maybe there is a failure in their life and your wisdom can help them see the purpose and silver lining. Sometimes wisdom guides you to just sit next to your kid and wrap your arm around them. Pray for wisdom.

Let me remind you and reinforce this, wisdom requires knowledge. If you are not engaged and mindful of your children, you will never possess the wisdom they need from you.

So be engaged today, make mental notes about your children, pray for wisdom, and allow God to guide you in using it for your child's benefit.

Your Fellow Father,
Anthony

Today's Step:

In addition to gaining wisdom through prayer and the word, another great way to grow in wisdom is to talk to another dad about experiences. Contact a dad and set up breakfast, lunch, dinner, or coffee.

Notes

Our Father is Peaceful

Isaiah 9:6 (NIV) - For to us a child is born, to us a son is given, and the government will be on his shoulders. And he will be called Wonderful Counselor, Mighty God, Everlasting Father, Prince of Peace.

When we think about God as being peaceful, we can consider a few factors.

First, he is peaceful in his approach. The Bible tells us he is slow to wrath and quick to mercy.

Second, he is at peace wholly. There is not chaos in God that makes him respond erratically.

Lastly, God is so full of peace that it is something that he dispenses and gives to us.

None of us will ever strip him of his title as the Prince of Peace, but we can certainly be peaceful like our Father. Just as long as we receive peace from him.

Peace requires knowledge. Think back to when Jesus was sleeping on the ship during the storm. The disciples feared they were going to die but Jesus kept sleeping. When they frantically woke him up, he did not join in their terror. Jesus had peace because he knew he could simply speak to the storm.

We do not have knowledge like that but we know the one who does. Just like we read in Psalm 46, we can be still in the middle of the chaos because we know God is sovereign and that he will be praised by all.

There is a good chance you have got chaos and uncertainty in your life. Stop leaning on your own understanding, start trusting in God's, and express gratitude for the goodness in your life. If you'll do that, you will receive peace from him that transcends your understanding.

Once you have peace, you can talk to your kids with more patience. You can smile over spilled milk instead of losing your cool. Most of all, you can show your kids that even if when times are tough, peace is available.

Lead with peace so that you can lead them to peace.

Your Fellow Father,
Anthony

Today's Step:

Thankfulness is your ticket to peace. Write down 7 things you are thankful for and tell your wife, kids, and at least one other person why you are thankful for them.

Notes

Our Father is Knowledgeable

Psalm 139:1 (NLT) - O LORD, you have examined my heart and know everything about me.

God's knowledge is all encompassing. He knows the end from the beginning and declares what will be way before it happens (Isaiah 46:9-10). Knowledge like that, is unattainable for us. However, our Father does model a knowledge we can aspire to have as dads; an intimate and detailed knowledge of our children.

We read, throughout the psalms, that God has an in-depth and personal knowledge of the heart, mind, and even the intent of individuals. God has taken the time to study and search us, so much so that he knows the number of hairs on our head (Luke 12:7), as well as what we need before we ask for it (Matthew 6:8).

In the latter portion of John 1, we find the story of Nathanael. Philip finds him and is ecstatic to tell him they have found the Messiah. Nathanael expresses skepticism because Philip mentioned Jesus coming from Nazareth, but he follows along to meet this so-called Messiah.

When Jesus sees Nathanael, he makes a comment about him which prompts Nathanael to ask Jesus, "how do you know me?" Jesus tells Nathanael, "I saw you while you were still under the fig tree before Philip called you."

We may not be able to see quite like our Father, but we have the ability to pay attention and see where our kids are in life. Like God, we must search for these things, which implies action and intentionality.

Our kids will not always come to us with new information about how they feel, what they have done, or what they have encountered, but if we, like Jesus, will be intentional about knowing our kids, we can do for our kids what Jesus did for Nathanael.

I want you to be intentional and proactive about knowing your children. Please hear me on this. While you should be aware of what your kids are doing, I am not prompting you to do this with the intent of finding out their secrets or mistakes. I want you to become knowledgeable about what they like. Where do they like to go? What do they like to eat? What do they have fun doing? What are their dreams? Having a knowledge of those things gives you access to serve them and help them in a greater capacity. You must know your kids.

Start paying attention. Take time to be around them so you can watch, observe, and take notes. You are in your child's life to lead them and to disciple them. Leadership and discipleship do not come in a one-size fits all form. Take the knowledge you gain and ask yourself, "How can I use this knowledge of my child to better lead and disciple them?"

Your Fellow Father,
Anthony

Today's Step:

Record one thing you notice or observe about your kid today. How can this knowledge be useful in your hand to greater enable you to serve them?

Notes

Our Father is a Leader

Psalm 23 (ESV) - The Lord is my shepherd; I shall not want. He makes me lie down in green pastures. He leads me beside still waters. He restores my soul. He leads me in paths of righteousness for his name's sake. Even though I walk through the valley of the shadow of death, I will fear no evil, for you are with me; your rod and your staff, they comfort me. You prepare a table before me in the presence of my enemies; you anoint my head with oil; my cup overflows. Surely goodness and mercy shall follow me all the days of my life, and I shall dwell in the house of the Lord forever.

This may be the most popular passage of scripture in our generation. It is a passage we go to in order to remind ourselves that God is with us. It is also a passage that displays our Father's leadership.

God, like a shepherd, walks with us through life helping us find rest and helping us navigate adversity. There are moments we are lead to places that bring us rest. There are other moments where we are lead through opposition and struggle. Through it all, God is faithful to lead us.

I want to highlight one aspect of our Father's leadership portrayed in this psalm. The language associated with adversity is something we can grab hold to in a very practical way. We read that he sets a table in the middle of the struggle and there we are blessed and reminded of purpose.

As a dad, I know you want to lead your kids to places of rest and enjoyment, but there are times you will need to lead them through challenges. Life has its ebbs and flows but when things get dark, there is something I want you to remember; the table.

The table is a staple piece in your house. It should be a safe space where love flows. Your table provides more than food for physical hunger, but also substance for the soul. As you lead your children through difficult situations, use the table.

I want you to be intentional about sitting down with your kids to just talk to them. Think about how you can take your table and transform it into a place that when your kid leaves, they are reminded that you are with them in life.

Leadership encompasses many qualities and attributes, but leadership like our Father's involves a table. You will be leading the way and paving a path, but do not forget to invite your kids to take a seat with you at the table.

Your Fellow Father,
Anthony

Today's Step:

Grab a snack or a treat of some sort and invite your kid(s) to have a seat with you at the table. You can talk, laugh, or play a game but make sure you spend time with them at the table today.

Notes

Our Father Is Light

1 John 1:5 (NIV) - This is the message we have heard from him and declare to you: God is light; in him there is no darkness at all.

In the event you are sporting a dadbod, fear not. This is not about "light" in terms of weight. Our Father is light in terms of illumination within a context of good.

Take a look back at the creation story. The earth was dark and chaotic, but then the word went forth and became light. Following this light, we begin to see the goodness that was there. Hidden by the darkness and chaos was a world with beautiful potential.

All of this was seen and identified because of the light. The light paved the way and the light continued to make growth possible.

I want you to be light to your kids. You should relate with them in such a way that you spotlight their goodness. When your children are with you, they should be able to see the good in themselves. This is something that you start when they are young but it remains just as important as they mature. Your light continues to shine helping them see there is goodness in themselves.

So in a practical sense, this starts with you identifying their goodness, personality, and talents. Then you spotlight these components so that they become obvious and blatant to your children.

My oldest, as young as five, wanted to be mature and independent. I remember walking into his room one morning to discover he had taken his National Geographic volcano and started it by himself.

He couldn't read all of the instructions but he could follow the pictures. This was something his mother and I told him he would have to do with us, but to my surprise, he was doing great without us.

As a light to my son, I remind him that he can do it, whatever it may be. He has the knowledge to figure things out and to tackle projects that might be a bit beyond him.

Be a light to your children. Find the goodness and strength in them, and shine so bright on your findings that they see them too.

Your Fellow Father,
Anthony

Today's Step:

Highlight something positive about your kid(s) today. Look beyond the surface level and illuminate the true attribute. Then help your children see it too.

Notes

Our Father is Patient

2 Peter 3:9 (NIV) - The Lord is not slow in keeping his promise, as some understand slowness. Instead he is patient with you, not wanting anyone to perish, but everyone to come to repentance.

Of all of the attributes of our Father, this is one that I am personally so thankful for. I can look back through my life and see mistake after mistake and poor decision after poor decision, but God exercised patience with me. Technically, our Father did this for all of us. The act of the cross was an act of patience. God made provision for us, even though we were not really looking for it. God was willing to act in advance and wait for us to respond.

A beautiful portrayal of this is seen in Luke 15, with the father of the prodigal son. This dad was willing to be patient concerning his son's development. He knew his son was not ready. He knew his son was setting out to make a huge mistake. He also knew that was probably a lesson and experience his younger son needed.

This dad was patient in waiting for his son to learn his lesson. He was not waiting around so that he could utter the famous words, "I told you so," he was waiting to help him. Knowing his son was about to learn a hard lesson, he waited for the opportunity to run to his aide and to lift him up.

As men and fathers, we are innately gifted with a desire to fix problems right away. When our wives or children come to us with an issue, we are quick to fire back with a solution. However, sometimes that is not the best approach. Sometimes what our children really need from us is patience. They need us to wait and watch. Because if we always step in and solve their problems, they will always be dependent upon us.

In addition, it is important for you to remember that no one gets it right the first time. Our children need time to make mistakes in order to learn. If you attempt to rush that, you cripple them, and all to appease your selfish desire for convenience. Be patient with your children and allow them to learn from experience and mistakes.

Also, you need to be patient with their process. There are lessons that you have taught them that they are not capable of understanding or appreciating yet. They need to grow up, get married, have kids of their own, and experience life to fully comprehend the wisdom you have poured into them.

Finally, watch and wait for their brokenness. Some mistakes will be harder than others. Some failures will motivate them to quit and cause them to feel worthless. Wait for those moments and then run to them. You do not ever need to tell them that you were right, and they were wrong. Running to their aide is never about stroking your ego. It is exclusively about helping them.

Remember, you are in their life to point them to God so that he can direct their path. Trust that God will do what he has always succeeded in doing. When the challenging times come, be patient, and know that God is at work.

Your Fellow Father,
Anthony

Today's Step:

Patience is a fruit of the Spirit. A faithful relationship with God will help with this. However, the practical step you need to implement is pausing and taking a breath. Your kids will inevitably do something today that is frustrating or blatantly wrong. Before you jump in, react, and correct, pause, take a breath to calm yourself, and then consider what to do.

Notes

The Next Step on the Path

I hope you have been able to clearly see your identity as a dad. I pray that change has already prevailed in your life and that it has positively impacted your relationship with your children. But now that you have reached the end of this devotional, what are you to do?

Continue to devote yourself to God. Prayer needs to be an everyday part of your life. You have access to talk to our Father and to learn from him. Please do that.

Stay in the word because it is alive. If you continue to read the Bible, you will continue to learn. Passages that you are familiar with still have the ability to speak to you in new ways. Be a man of the word.

Less important than those, go through this devotional again. This was never intended to be a thirty-day crash course that you never need to revisit. Fatherhood is a lifelong journey. You will continue to learn and to develop as a dad. If this devotional aides you in refocusing on your identity as a father, keep using it.

Know that you are not alone on this journey. Your Father cares about you and your development as a father. Other dads, such as myself, are here to support you and to walk this path with you.

If you need help, please feel free to email me at fatheringourfuture@gmail.com. If you want to keep learning, subscribe to Fathering Our Future wherever you listen to podcasts and visit www.fatheringourfuture.com.

The Final Assignment

Remember at the beginning where I explained what it means to devote? Now that you have completed this devotional, I want you to write down what has most resonated with you. Take your time. Include details. Write down specific examples based on where you currently are in life. Just remember to take your time.

Upon completing your thoughts, I want you to set a reminder in your phone for no longer than one year from today. I want you to come back and read, at least your key takeaways, so you can see how much you have grown.

Notes

Made in the USA
Monee, IL
23 August 2024